The most excellent book of

how to be a

clown

Catherine Perkins

Stargazer Books

New edition 2007
© Aladdin Books Ltd 1996

Designed and produced by
Aladdin Books Ltd

*New edition published in the
United States in 2007 by*
Stargazer Books
c/o The Creative Company
123 South Broad Street
P.O. Box 227
Mankato, Minnesota 56002

Editor
Katie Roden
Design David West Children's
Book Design
Designer
Edward Simkins

Printed in the
United States

**Library of
Congress Cataloging-
in-Publication Data**
Perkins, Catherine.
How to be a clown /
by Catherine Perkins.
p. cm. -- (Most
excellent book of--)
Originally published:
The most excellent book
of how to be a clown.
Brookfield, Conn. :
Copper Beech
Books, 1996.
Includes index.
ISBN 978-1-59604-124-0
1. Clowning--Juvenile
literature. 2. Clowns--
Juvenile literature. I.
Perkins, Catherine. Most excellent
book of how to be a clown. II.
Title. III. Series.

GV1828.P46 1996
791.3'3--dc22

2005057622

CONTENTS

INTRODUCTION

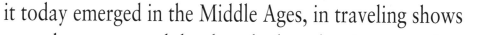

Clowns have entertained the world for centuries. The first records of clowns date from about 3000 B.C., in ancient Egyptian writings, and they were popular in ancient Greece (*right*) and Rome. The clown as we know it today emerged in the Middle Ages, in traveling shows and at court, and developed when the circus was invented, in the 18th century.

This book will tell you all you need to know to develop a spectacular clown character and act. Look for these symbols to help you:

★ tells you the basic things that every clown should know.

✔ has tips to help you perfect your craft.

Read on, and in no time at all...you'll be a clown!

The Pierrot, shown above in a 1920s drawing, first developed in 16th-century Europe and continues to be popular today. Movie clowns like Charlie Chaplin (1889–1977, right) entertained the world throughout the 20th century.

Choosing your CLOWN

Find a character to suit your personality.

★ *Every clown has a different character and way of behaving. The first thing you need to do is to invent a character that you feel comfortable with. These are the most common types of clowns; use them to help you develop a unique character.*

The Auguste

This clown is the traditional "buffoon" character, with zany clothes and colorful makeup. The auguste (pronounced "aw-goost") is clumsy and cheerful, and plays silly jokes. He or she might play a musical instrument (but not very well!). The main features of the auguste are:

1 Exaggerated makeup with lots of colors (*see pages 10–11*).

2 Bright clothes – often an oversized business suit.

3 Huge shoes, a colorful wig, and a silly hat.

4 Clumsy movements, which usually have extremely messy results!

The Whiteface

This clown is much quieter and more refined, with a less colorful costume. The whiteface can be very serious, and is often the butt of the auguste's jokes! He or she always tries to look dignified – but this isn't usually very easy. The main features of the whiteface are:

1 Mainly white makeup, with small features (*see page 13*).

2 An oversized, one-color costume. This may look like a pair of big pajamas with a ruff.

3 A small cap or hat.

4 More serious, dignified behavior.

★ *Make sure your clown character suits your personality. If you are naturally quiet, a whiteface character might be better for you; if you like playing jokes and being noisy, try an auguste. Your clown can be silent and communicate only in mime (see pages 6–7), or can be loud and talkative. If you play a musical instrument, you can use this in your act. You can also play CDs that are suitable for your character.*

Mime and CLOWNING HINTS

The basics for a crazy clown show!

★ *Remember these mime tips and your clown act will be hilarious!*

Silly Moves

Clowns are funny because they are larger than life, so all your gestures should be big and clear. Invent your own silly way of walking and exaggerate all your movements.

The Audience

An important part of clowning is the effect of your act on the audience. When you perform an action, look at your audience with a clear, exaggerated expression.

Expressing Yourself

Clowns wear lots of makeup so that their faces can be seen clearly. They use big facial expressions to show their feelings or tell a story. If you want to show the audience that you are happy, give them a HUGE smile. To show surprise, open your eyes and mouth wide. Show all your reactions to events as clearly as possible.

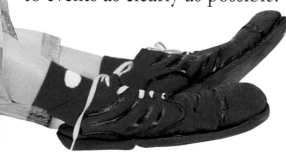

The Art of Mime

Mime, or the art of expressing yourself with your face and body rather than words, is important for every clown. If you watch mime artists such as Marcel Marceau (*below*), you will see that they use exaggerated expressions and gestures. Marceau is so skilled that he can perform entire stories without speaking at all.

The Clown's COSTUME

Now you need an outfit to suit your clown character.

Vest and shirt
You need a vest or jacket, to cover hidden tricks. See if you can borrow an old one and decorate it with colors and patterns. Find an old T-shirt or shirt and decorate it with fabric paints or cut-out shapes to suit your character.

Gloves
Some clowns wear white or colored gloves.

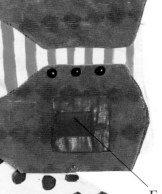

Hat and wig
Most joke shops sell cheap hats and wigs, but you can also make your own. Use a cone of brightly colored cardboard for a hat, and stick on colorful wool or curls of paper for wacky hair.

Bow tie
This is essential for the auguste; the whiteface wears a ruffled collar (see page 5). Make these from crêpe paper and attach them with safety pins.

Fake pocket (see page 28)

Pants

Big, baggy pants are an essential part of a clown's kit! See if you can borrow an old pair from an adult, and decorate them with patches, shapes, and bright colors. Roll them up at the bottom, and hold them up with crazy suspenders if necessary.

Use Your Imagination!

These are just a few basic tips – now you should try to adapt your costume to suit your own clown character. If you have decided to be a whiteface clown, look at the costume on page 5 to give you some ideas. If you wear glasses, try decorating your frames with bright cardboard shapes to match your costume. You could make a wig from tinsel, to give your act extra sparkle!

Socks

Find the wackiest pair you can, or decorate some old socks with fabric paints or stick-on shapes and glitter.

Shoes

Big shoes will help your silly movements! Borrow old ones from an adult and decorate them. Slip a pair of your own shoes inside. Pad them with paper to stop your feet from slipping out.

Your Clown's FACE

Use this face as a basis for your own design.

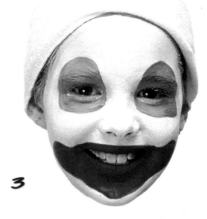

3 Add color around your eyes. Powder again, using different brushes for the colors and the white.

❶ Paint a white base. (*see page 13 for the makeup you need) and powder it.*

3

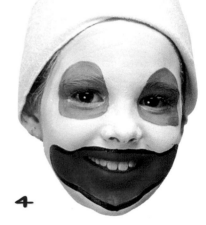

4

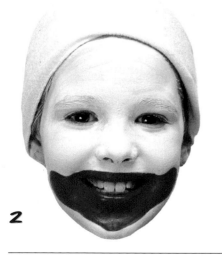

2 Carefully paint the red areas, such as your mouth. Give a big smile in the mirror, and follow its shape with the red makeup.

2

4 Using the eyeliner, carefully outline your red mouth area.

5 Carefully outline the rest of the colored areas with the eyeliner.

6 Add some eyebrows. Powder again with two brushes.

✔ *Once you have made a basic face, you can add your own details. Turn to the next page for some more ideas.*

A Nose for Clowning

A red nose is a vital part of a clown's kit. The whiteface has a painted nose; augustes wear fake ones. Most joke shops sell noses. You can make one from a sponge ball soaked in red food coloring, with a slit or elastic to hold it on.

More Crazy FACES

 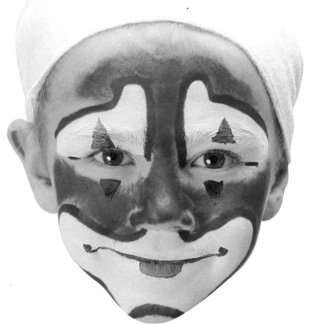

❶ The Sad Clown

This is a white base with small areas of color and black detail. Pull a sad face, and use your makeup to emphasize the shapes it makes.

❷ The Cheery Clown

This is the opposite of the basic face on pages 10–11. First, paint your eyes and mouth white. Add colors on your face and finish off with black details.

A Clown's Essential Makeup Kit

You can buy special clown makeup, but face paints are just as good. You will need white makeup as a base, a selection of colors and a black eyeliner (the "pen"-style ones are the best). Use a pale powder and apply it with soft brushes. Remove the makeup with baby oil or cold cream and cotton balls.

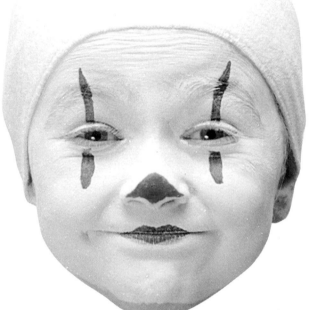

3 The Whiteface

This design is based on that of the classic Pierrot whiteface clown (*see pages 3 and 5*). Paint a white base first, then add a few delicate black details and a small red nose.

Funny BODY

An excellent way to begin your act!

★ *Get into position before the audience arrive.*

1 Begin the show with your arms pulled into your sleeves and your legs slightly bent in your baggy pants, so that your hands and feet are hidden.

2 Push your left hand out of your sleeve, then use it to pull your right hand out slowly. Your arms will seem to get longer and longer!

3 Slowly straighten your right leg, keeping the left slightly bent, so your right leg looks longer than the left. Repeat this the other way round.

✔ *Make these tricks even funnier by expressing great surprise as your arms and legs seem to get longer!*

The WEIGHT LIFTER

What a strong clown!

★ *Instructions for making the dumbbells are on page 29. Put them in position before your show, so that no one knows how light they are!*

1 Flex your muscles to the audience, to show them how strong you are. The more exaggerated your movements are, the funnier your act will be.

2 Bend down to pick up the dumbbells – but pretend that they are too heavy! To do this, keep your arms still and show all the strain of lifting in your body and face.

3 Keep trying to lift the dumbbells, getting more and more exasperated. Finally, pretend to give up – just pick up the dumbbells and walk away!

✔ *It is a good idea to practice your mimes in front of a mirror until they look convincing.*

2

3

Juggle AWAY!

An essential skill for every clown!

★ *Stare at 2 points on either side of your face, 1 ft (30cm) in front of you. Watch these points, not the bags or your hands. Instructions for making the bags are on page 30.*

Single Bag ❶ Hold the bag in your right hand. Throw it to the left-hand point and catch it in your left hand.
2 Throw it to the right. Practice until you hit the points every time. Don't lift your hands to catch the bag: let it fall into your palms.

Two Bags **3** Hold a bag in each hand. Throw the right-hand bag. When it reaches the left-hand point, throw the left-hand bag.
4 Catch the first bag in your left hand and the other in your right. Practice until you can catch the bags every time.
5 Try the same thing, but start with your left hand this time. Don't stop!

Three bags 6 Take one bag in each hand and imagine you have a third bag in your right hand. **7** Juggle the bags, starting with the right. When the left-hand bag hits its point, pretend to throw the imaginary bag to the left point then catch the left-hand bag in your right hand. Practice this rhythm. **8** Try with a real bag! Always throw the bag that is in your hand before catching another one.

✔ *If you drop a bag while you are performing, don't worry! Think up some jokes to cover any mistakes. If you find it hard to juggle with bags, try using handkerchiefs.*

The BRICK WALL

A classic mime that never fails to impress an audience!

★ *Use very exaggerated movements and faces to make this act hilarious!*

1 Walk forward, and pretend to bump into an invisible wall (shown here as a guide).

2 "Feel" your way along the wall, moving your hands from side to side and up and down.

✔ *Practice your mime on a real wall. Make sure the position of the invisible wall does not change.*

3 As you feel your way, pretend that you find a door handle and open a door. Walk through.

4 You've made it! Take a big bow to the audience in celebration, then turn and start to walk away from them.

5 CRASH! You forgot about the wall! Pretend to bump into it again, and fall down in an exaggerated way.

✔ *Keep your hands relaxed and your fingers slightly bent.*

✔ *As you move, spread your palms as if pressing on a flat surface.*

✔ *You could adapt this mime to pretend that you are trapped in a box.*

Even More MIMES

Have your audience in stitches!

❶ The Terrified Tightrope Walker
Imagine that there is a rope on
the floor (shown
here as a
guide). Mime a
balance pole (shown as a guide)
and walk carefully along the line,
in a heel-to-toe step. Use your
mime skills to show how
nervous you are!

2 A Windy Day Mime being hit by a huge gust
of wind. Look up and open your hand to
show that you have felt a drop of rain, then
open your umbrella. Mime that it gets caught
by the wind and tries to pull you into the air!

3 **The Stubborn Balloon** Blow up a balloon. As you start to walk away with it, pretend that it will not move, and try to push it. Create this illusion by keeping your arms still, with your elbows bent. Show all the effort of pushing in your body and face. Now pretend that the balloon starts to float upward, pulling you with it. Try to hold it down. Pretend to struggle furiously with it and to get more and more annoyed...until you pull out a pin and burst it!

A *Clown's* BEST FRIEND

This invisible dog has a mind of its own!

★ *Instructions for making a leash are on page 31. Decide how big your "dog" is, and keep the leash at this height.*

1 Mime that you are trying to walk your dog, but it won't budge!

2 Pretend to pull the leash. Keep your arms and the leash still, and show lots of effort in your body and face.

3 Suddenly, the dog decides to go for a run! Show this by quickly jerking the leash across your body and leaning forward as if you are being pulled.

4 Run across the stage, leaning forward and with the leash in front of you. Keep trying to stop by pulling the leash, then jerk forward again.

5 Pretend that you are pulled right off the stage!

✔ *To make your act finish with a real bang, put a pile of old saucepans just out of sight of the audience.*

When you are dragged away, use the pans to make an ear-splitting crash!

3

4

5

Confetti BUCKET

Beware of this clumsy clown!

★ *Instructions for making the bucket are on page 30.*

❶ Hold the bucket so your fingers touch the top of the bag and hold it open. Pretend to pour the water into the bucket. In fact, you should pour it carefully into the bag.

2 Secretly close the bag and seal the tape firmly.

3 Walk forward with the bucket.

4 Pretend to trip, and empty the bucket over the audience!

✔ *Make sure the bag is sealed securely. Use your acting skills to convince the audience that the bucket is full of water!*

Confetti SNEEZE

This character has a colorful cold!

★ *Wrap some bright confetti in a big handkerchief, and keep it in your pocket during your act.*

1 At a certain point in your act, stop what you are doing or saying and pretend that you are going to sneeze. Use exaggerated movements and noises to convince the audience that it will be enormous!

2 Fumble frantically in your pocket and pull out the handkerchief. Make sure that no confetti falls out at this stage.

3 Open the handkerchief between your hands, so the confetti is on top (but not visible to the audience).

4 Throw your head back, then mime a huge sneeze. Blow the confetti off the handkerchief as you do so.

The DECORATOR

How will you get out of this sticky situation?

★ *Stick pieces of double-sided tape on to the brush and paper to make them stick to your hands!*

❶ Pretend that you are a decorator, arriving to paper a wall, carrying a roll of wallpaper and a bucket containing a brush. Put the paper on a table and the bucket on the floor.

2 Unroll the paper, holding on to both ends.

3 Turn to pick the brush off the floor, letting go of the paper. It will roll up again. Turn around and see this, sigh, then put the brush in the bucket again. Unroll the paper, turn to get the brush...and let the same thing happen all over again! Repeat this sequence several times.

4 Bright idea! Put the bucket on one end of the paper and hold the other.

5 Start "pasting" the paper. Dip the brush into the bucket. As you do so, put your hand on the tape so it gets stuck!

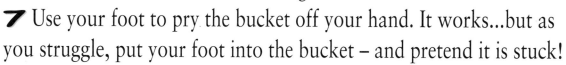

6 Put the brush into the bucket. Pretend that your other hand gets stuck to the bucket!

7 Use your foot to pry the bucket off your hand. It works...but as you struggle, put your foot into the bucket – and pretend it is stuck!

8 Try to pull the bucket off your foot. As you do so, grab the tape on the brush, so it gets stuck too!

9 This really is the final straw! All you can do is shrug at the audience...and hobble away!

✔ *To make this act even funnier, ask the audience to shout out when the paper rolls up again.*

Laundry DAY

A clown with bottomless pockets!

★ *See the next page for instructions to make the clothesline. To make a fake pocket you need: a large square of material; a needle and thread; scissors.*

1. *Cut a slit in your vest.*
2. *Sew the material over the slit.*
3. *Tuck the clothesline into your pants, with one end of it sticking over your waistband and into the fake pocket.*

❙ Tell the audience that you will do a trick with a piece of string. Reach into your pocket and grab the end of the clothesline.

2 Slowly pull the line out of your pocket, expressing surprise as each object appears.

✔ *Try this using other objects, like magic wands, big handkerchiefs, or bunches of paper flowers.*

The PROPS

Everything you need for a spectacular act!

Dumbbells
★ *You will need: a long piece of wood dowelling; two balloons; black paint; sticky tape.*

1 Blow up the balloons until they are about the same size.

2 Stick the balloons to the ends of the dowelling.

3 Paint the balloons and the dowelling with the black paint.

The Clothesline
★ *You will need: a long piece of string; bright clothes, like socks and T-shirts; colorful handkerchiefs; silly underpants (you can make these from felt); safety pins.*

1 Arrange the clothes and handkerchiefs on the clothesline and secure them with safety pins.

2 Put the underpants at the end and pull them out last, looking embarrassed – your act will finish hilariously!

More PROPS

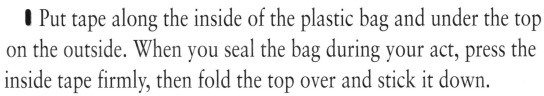

Confetti Bucket

★ *You will need: a plastic bucket; strong glue; a strong, see-through, watertight plastic bag; double-sided sticky tape; confetti or scraps of colorful torn-up paper.*

1 Put tape along the inside of the plastic bag and under the top on the outside. When you seal the bag during your act, press the inside tape firmly, then fold the top over and stick it down.

2 Stick the bag with glue to the inside of the bucket just below the rim, with the open mouth of the bag facing upward. MAKE SURE THAT THE BAG IS ATTACHED VERY SECURELY AT THE TOP AND BOTTOM.

3 Put the confetti into the bottom of the bucket.

✔ *Decorate all your props to match your costume and the personality of your clown. As you practice your act, think of new ways to make it even more spectacular. You could use glitter or luminous paints, or make oversized props.*

Juggling Bags

★ *You will need:*
two pairs of old thin socks; dried
beans; needle and thread; scissors.

❚ Fill the socks with the dried beans, until they are just big enough to fit comfortably into the palm of your hand. Do not fill them too tightly, or they might burst if you drop them.

2 Carefully sew up the tops of the socks with two rows of small, tight stitches, to make them as strong and secure as possible.

Dog Leash

★ *You will*
need: a long piece of
wire; felt; strong glue;
scissors; a small buckle.

❚ Bend the end of the wire into a large loop. Twist it at the join so that it sticks out at an angle from the straight part of the wire.

2 Cut the felt into two strips, both the same length as the loop.

3 Stick the felt around the loop. Stick more felt to the long part of the wire if you want it to match the loop.

4 Stick the buckle onto the front of the loop.

5 Decorate the leash to match your costume.

Clown WORDS

Audience The people who watch your show.

Buffoon A clumsy, noisy clown character.

Character The personality of the type of clown you choose.

Exaggerate To emphasize something by making it larger than life.

Props All the objects that you use during your act.

Ruff A large collar with many folds, usually made of cotton or lace.

Keep on CLOWNING!

If you want to learn more about clowning, many towns have circus schools and workshops. Watching clowns on TV is a good way to get ideas, or you could work out an act with your friends.

INDEX

Picture credits
(t-top, m-middle, b-bottom)
All pictures by Roger Vlitos, except: 3t - Ancient Art & Architecture Collection; 3m - Mary Evans Picture Library; 3b, 7 - Frank Spooner Pictures